JAMES GANDOLFINI

A Genius, Demons, and The Sopranos.

Gist Hub

Table of contents

Chapter 1: The Birth of a Television Legend

David Chase had worked in television for over twenty years, logging time on shows like The Rockford Files and Northern Exposure, before conceiving his own series centered on the mafia. But this would be not a cops and robbers production featuring tidy resolutions where the bad guys always lost in the end. No, Chase envisioned a deeper exploration of the psyche of one mobster and the families—both criminal and personal—he navigated. He wanted to probe what drove some to engage in violence, betrayal, manipulation, and corruption as a way of life. The show would break boundaries with an anti-hero protagonist who was complex, brutal, vulnerable, and relatable all at once.

As a New Jersey native himself, Chase set the production in the Garden State, focusing on fictional mob boss Tony Soprano and his inner circle operating out of Essex County as he managed family tensions, power struggles among crews, and periodic outbreaks of violence that came with the territory.

But Tony would have more going on beneath the ruthless veneer as the central premise involved him entering psychotherapy due to escalating anxiety attacks that landed him in the hospital. This allowed an analytical glimpse into Tony's psyche, including an overbearing mother that shaped his warped view of life and near-constant feelings of panic despite occupying the top position in his crew.

Chase secured support for the concept, originally titled The Family, through production companies Brillstein Entertainment Partners and HBO. The team believed airing on premium cable would grant the artistic freedom and lack of censorship needed to fulfill Chase's ambitions for raw yet nuanced storytelling.

But they knew that landing the lead role was absolutely crucial to achieving their lofty goals for the program. They required a tremendously skilled actor who could capture all the tightropes Tony walked between callous mob boss, vulnerable patient seeking answers through therapy, hot-tempered and violent loose cannon, shrewd strategist, conflicted Catholic, affectionate family man, and consummate actor pretending that nothing lurked beneath the successful owner of a local waste management company.

The search initially focused on established film stars but ultimately brought Chase and the production team to James Gandolfini, who possessed thoroughly convincing dramatic chops on screen but found himself pigeonholed in tough guy and henchmen roles at just 36 years old. His talent and presence leaped off the screen, but he had yet to land a star-making turn matching his abilities.

Still, glimpses in films like True Romance and Terminal Velocity along with a steady slate of television credits provided enough proof for Chase that he had located his Tony Soprano after an extensive audition process. Several elements of his background also harmonized perfectly with the Italian-American mob boss character, lending further authenticity.

Gandolfini grew up in a working class Italian neighborhood in New Jersey where run-ins with real wiseguys were not uncommon. He spent time accompanying his father, who oversaw facilities and janitorial work at various New York City schools, absorbing Big Apple food culture through meals at pizza parlors and Italian restaurants that would resurface when getting into character.

His volatile and explosive tendencies demonstrated on set foreshadowed the mercurial temper and menacing outbursts Tony Soprano would unleash. Gandolfini inhabited rejection and struggles early on, dropping out of Rutgers and dealing with bouts of substance abuse while finding little traction professionally during his 20s. But he later rediscovered his passion for acting and steadily accrued credits that laid the foundations for bigger opportunities.

When the lengthy, arduous auditions concluded, Chase and the producers knew they had uncovered a rare talent perfectly attuned to realizing their mafia antihero. Upon landing the career-defining role, Gandolfini fully immersed himself into Tony's world. He remained in character on set, cultivated meaningful bonds with cast mates that translated on screen, and always steeped himself in the emotions, motivations, and internal struggles defining Tony ahead of shooting scenes. Gandolfini soaked up the character until fully inhabiting him in an uncanny fusion that made Tony Soprano truly feel like one of the most fully formed figures ever brought to life on television screens.

Of course, Chase would go on to be credited as a creative visionary who changed expectations for television writing, directing, freedom of content, and exploration of the soul that shows could achieve. The crystalline writing and film production also won mountains of praise. But at the center of it all resided Gandolfini's transcendent acting that lifted the medium to new heights starting with the pilot and never let up across a staggering 86 total episodes. Without his gleaming talent delivering the goods early and often, the show simply could never have become what it did.

For an actor with supporting credits to his name and no leading parts under his belt, Gandolfini grabbed hold of the once-in-a-lifetime opportunity with both hands. The result was an iconic performance that indelibly shaped The Sopranos into the cultural touchstone that launched the 21st century's golden age of deeply cinematic television. Tony Soprano lived and breathed in fully tangible form through Gandolfini, down to every register of his gravelly voice. And Chase had his perfect vessel to manifest his grand vision.

Chapter 2: Magic and Mayhem on Set

The Sopranos pilot sparked electrifying chemistry between the sterling ensemble cast, led by Gandolfini's volcanic performance as Tony Soprano. HBO executives knew they had something special, greenlighting an entire season order. As production ramped up, Chase harnessed Gandolfini's immense yet raw talent to realize his vision for the show, capturing magic on screen while mayhem brewed behind the scenes.

Gandolfini anchored his scenes with commanding presence and emotional authenticity, buoyed by a colorful supporting cast. As Carmela, Edie Falco perfectly channeled theGroundshattering Television 76 exhausted yet resilient mob wife. A young Michael Imperioli brought Christopher Moltisanti to life with hunger and intensity. Tony Sirico's turn as the loyal yet unhinged Paulie

Walnuts stole scenes. And Nancy Marchand's Livia Soprano delivered cunning toxicity as Tony's mother. Chase gave his players creative freedom in finding their characters, fostering rich development beyond what existed on paper.

Showcasing both sweeping cinematic style and gritty realism, Chase directed the pilot more like a mini-movie, a creative swing for the fences. He wanted to grab audiences by the throat while subverting expectations, particularly through Dr. Melfi's arc played by Lorraine Bracco. Just as Tony opened his psyche and vulnerabilities to his therapist, revealing hanging questions about nature versus nurture in shaping one's path, Chase extended the same intimate access to viewers.

Peeling back the layers of this complex central character required time and revelation doled out across episodes, but Gandolfini reeled fans in from minute one. His turn as Tony granted the character numerous dimensions when a more superficial portrayal would have centered steadfast toughness and unwavering criminal ruthlessness. But behind the steely veneer lies endless nuances.

Gandolfini municipality traversed Tony Soprano's various roles with finesse: violent intimidator navigating threats from New York crews and the FBI; doting husband struggling to reconcile infidelities given warped concepts about gender dynamics gleaned from his toxic upbringing; loving father who espouses wanting a better life for his children than the mafia path he chose; tortured soul self-medicating anxiety with alcohol and strip club dalliances due to an inability to openly address the source of anguish or meaningfully change; headstrong captain issuing orders and demands but never asking for input from those tasked with carrying them out; conflicted Catholic who envisions flames when life is over but rationalizes mortal sins to justify gruesome means on the way; and more.

With Gandolfini flawlessly oscillating between poles, lighting up synapses across regions of

Tony's amygdala, the first episodes of season one felt like catching lightning in a bottle creatively. Scenes popped with vivid authenticity while Chase actively avoided overused mob genre tropes in favor of psychological exploration. Flashes of violence and confrontation punctuated seasons of therapy breakthroughs, squabbles with Carmela, tension with his mother, and managing business. Loyalties and affections constantly shifted among his crew as well. Gandolfini's towering execution captured it all.

But behind the scenes, Gandolfini's reliance on drugs, alcohol, and more unhinged forms of stress release began taking a toll. He started missing call times, keeping the cast and crew waiting for hours before sauntering onto the set still half in the bag from the previous night's bender. Or he appeared drunk or severely hungover, unable to focus fully or control temperamental outbursts. When guests like Sirico visited Gandolfini's trailer to hash out how to refine scenes collaboratively, they encountered littered beer cans, remnants of substances, ashtrays overflowing with cigarettes.

Crew members knew alcohol allowed Gandolfini to decompress from inhabiting Tony's skin. But they saw consumption increasingly slide into darker territory. He began drinking not just beer but straight tequila and whiskey as early as 10am. Lines of coke appeared with greater frequency to rouse focus. Cast and crew started doubting his ability to deliver a usable first take, much less remember mark points. Yet when channels engaged, the inspired acting resumed as if flicking a switch. So they shouldered growing frustrations because Gandolfini represented the show's creative bedrock.

As the erratic behavior worsened, Gandolfini's co-stars grew less patient. Imperioli bristled when Gandolfini disappeared for a long lunch and returned obviously intoxicated. Falco fumed when he failed to learn lines on time, botching her ability to rehearse. He began lashing out unpredictably, sparking tensions. One flare up turned physical when Gandolfini violently slammed a refrigerator door and shattered its glass door after reading half-written scripts. After each outburst, he sheepishly apologized, vowing to curb the substances and instability but failing to truly alter course. The dynamic upset cast mates were forced to shoulder extra burdens.

Yet Gandolfini's charming charisma and bottomless generosity toward Sopranos' crew members undercut growing resentment. Every Friday without fail, he insisted HBO order sushi for everyone on set. And he gifted entire teams expensive watches or cash bonuses worth thousands at season wrap parties. So personal assistants, set designers, grips, camera operators, and more tolerated the unpredictable swings and frequent lateness through sheer loyalty even as it hindered filming.

Between the first and second seasons, HBO urged Gandolfini to enter rehab, terrified of losing their luminous star. When he refused, Chase and producers doubled down on accommodations to keep Gandolfini happy onset, including extended breaks. They treated gently to appease their brilliant yet troubled foundation. And for a while, it worked. Gandolfini managed just enough stability to prevent complete production derailment while summoning incredible performances.

Yet the drugs never fully disappeared as seasons wore on. Co-stars simmer seeing extreme fits followed by generous gifts when clear steps toward recovery never stick. For all the tedium his habits caused, the pure vigor Gandolfini poured into scenes still resulted in viewing unlike anything previously achieved on television. So the direction remained steady even amidst constant storms behind the camera. With Chase at the helm, The Sopranos captured episodic magic thanks to Gandolfini while managing his self-destructive mayhem backstage, at least for a spell.

Chapter 3: Struggling with Inner Demons

By The Sopranos' third season, Gandolfini's burgeoning fame and fortunes allowed greater indulgence in drugs, alcohol, and other vices now accessible in excess. His partying became legendary, with epic benders trailing into mornings after. Photos surfaced in tabloid rags of the star stumbling out of clubs, nursing bottles through bloodshot eyes. During a film shoot in Las Vegas, he disappeared on a four-day bender later unable to recall large gaps.

As Gandolfini sank deeper, his moods turned darker and more explosive on set. Small creative debates escalated without warning. Impatient outbursts left co-stars feeling attacked when scenes required additional takes to master. Things grew tense around the star constantly Fiery Eruptions 85 looking to numb inner anguish. The sparkling humor and easy rapport with castmates increasingly became replaced by isolating silences. He refused any personal questions, barricading prying eyes from the well of sadness he attempted to fill through external means.

While succeeding professionally, Gandolfini floundered personally. His first marriage crumbled from the weight of too much time apart and too many broken promises of sobriety. Custody disputes over his young son Michael grew bitter and painful. Despite fame and admirers, loneliness is haunted. Gandolfini kept even closest friends and collaborators at bay, internalizing whatever fueled the growing void.

The danger escalated during season four when repercussions intensified from reckless overindulgence. Gandolfini arrived on set with a bandaged face after a vicious brawl landed him in intensive care. Shooting halted for days. Tabloids later revealed an ugly strip club altercation involving drugs, prostitutes, thrown bottles and orbital bone surgery. HBO executives seized the moment, issuing non-negotiable demands for rehab before allowing a return.

So Gandolfini reluctantly agreed to treatments, determined to straighten up with so much professionally at stake. But surrounded by enablers and lacking meaningful system support upon release, sobriety quickly crumbled. Overdoses required two emergency room trips as Gandolfini's anguished reliance on illicit coping mechanisms raged beyond control.

The inability to pull himself from the tailspin despite near death experiences reflected immense internal pain no amount of external speechifying could quell. Still, HBO and managers tried desperately through interventions intended to make Gandolfini intimately face consequences in hopes of spurring change.

The first came orchestrated by HBO chief Chris Albrecht at his New Jersey home. But when

Gandolfini arrived to find a small crowd including family and friends, he angrily cursed the ambush before storming off into the night. A later hotel room attempt saw Gandolfini's team prepared to whisk him immediately to a private plane headed for rehab. But he barricaded himself in the bathroom after two minutes, refusing to emerge.

Each failed attempt further reinforced Gandolfini's fortress-like walls. Every passionate plea and breakdown of loved ones' heartache only seemed to steal his drive toward self-destruction. There existed a profound disconnect as he attended fine dining events, vacationed on yachts, and enjoyed every privilege while hopelessness persisted. No consequences or interventions could pierce whatever turmoil raged underneath.

By The Sopranos fifth season, skepticism mounted whether Gandolfini could physically or emotionally handle continuing Tony's complex arc. HBO CEO Chris Albrecht confessed to the show's crew that concerns over Gandolfini's basic survival grew daily. Network brass realized that despite insulating their troubled star, Gandolfini continued declining before their eyes.

Yet they also understood that his weekly acting high wire without a net – consistently nailing scenes while nursing lingering withdrawals, devastating depression, and intense anxiety – fueled the palpable authenticity that made Tony Soprano so relatable. Audiences experienced the character's rollercoaster because Gandolfini lived it too. Their tragic hero constantly tamped down panic attacks and cried for help behind a veneer of macho control. Like the actor portraying him, the character depended on vice to navigate internal chaos.

So producers treated cautiously, employing contingency plans to pick up slack but not daring intervention again for fear of losing Gandolfini for good. They held out hope that increased salary bonuses allowing more extensive breaks would provide enough relief between seasons.

But as cameras rolled on what would be The Sopranos final bow over 20 arduous months, grave uncertainty hung thick as Gandolfini's harrowed gaze grew more distant by the day.

The final episode 'Made in America' marked the end of an era on June 10, 2007. As the iconic closing scene faded abruptly to silence, so too did another chapter of Gandolfini's tumultuous life. With structured filming wrapped, familiar demons fast encroached the actor now lacking professional distraction. No one could predict what came next.

Chapter 4: The Crew's Loyalty Tested

The Sopranos crew experienced both extreme frustration and fondness for their flawed star Gandolfini. While late arrivals and compromised conditions tested patience, his warm charm still broke through. Many crew members became genuinely protective, fretting over Gandolfini's rapid deterioration in offline hours. They tried uplifting his spirits through lighthearted moments between takes.

Gandolfini also prioritized bonding with crews, considering them extended family. Every Friday without fail, he sent his assistant to order elaborate sushi dinners catered so everyone could enjoy together. Crew members fondly recount these rituals over post-shoot drinks and bonding.

The star also thoughtfully acknowledged the crew's solidarity despite disruptions tied to his issues. Each season wrapped, Gandolfini gifted team members expensive parting presents—designer watches, luggage sets, spa visits, and shopping sprees conveying his gratitude for their loyalty under trying circumstances.

These expressions of warmth from Gandolfini fueled crew members' resolve in standing firmly beside him. They became determined to help their flawed leader cross the finish line, paying tolerance forward through reliability, empathy and discretion.

However, Gandolfini's downward trajectories between seasons still produced hairy incidents requiring intensive damage control and enabling. His inner circle of handlers and assistants ran point on these cleanup efforts.

In one alarming case, Gandolfini disappeared for 96 hours on a drug binge during a film shoot. His team concocted a fictional story that the actor had departed on a bold humanitarian trip visiting and comforting families of fallen soldiers. This successfully quashed what would have otherwise been disastrous press.

In another terrifying instance, one of Gandolfini's assistants received a late night call saying he was in bad shape at a Manhattan hotel under dubious circumstances. The assistant arrived in a room in shambles – broken glass, overturned furniture, suspicious powders and no sign of the star. As he was scrambling trying to locate Gandolfini, sudden loud pounding came from inside the wall near the bathroom.

It turned out the disoriented actor had inexplicably punched and ripped away thick drywall before crawling inside the building's skeleton. He remained hunkered within the narrow, dangerous construction cavity unsure what happened prior. Had his assistant not shown up, dire possibilities loomed given Gandolfini's trapped predicament.

Careful extraction and discreet departure followed, enabling dangerous behavior patterns to continue with no broader awareness or consequences to force intervention.

This stark incident encapsulates the constant risk present beneath the surface during periods of production calm. Gandolfini's life hung perpetually in the balance while keeping up the facade driving HBO's crown jewel franchise. Everyone around him lived on the razor's edge.

Yet despite the turbulence, for those not bearing direct responsibility, loyalty toward the gifted yet deeply tortured soul prevailed. The crew became his fierce protectors, bailing Gandolfini out of compromising situations while shielding wider knowledge that may have forced career intervention. Gandolfini surely realized these allowances and displayed immense appreciation through gracious gestures.

But no gift or act of consideration could smooth the uneasy thrill ride as seasons churned on, uncertainty ever-present around the next hairpin turn. The question loomed whether their stoic leader could survive long enough to reach the destination before crashing catastrophically. It was a hell of a rollercoaster many stuck with to the white-knuckle end because despite everything, Gandolfini put magic on screen while showing real dimension behind the scenes when desire briefly overpowered darker impulses tearing him apart.

Chapter 5: The Iconic Legacy

The Sopranos garnered immense critical praise and awards attention, cementing Gandolfini as an acting tour de force. His inhabited portrayal of anxiety-prone mob boss Tony Soprano immediately entranced audiences. By channeling his own inner turmoil, Gandolfini brought groundbreaking emotional depth to an antihero character type historically portrayed in more straight-forward fashion.

Gandolfini won universal adoration for his weekly acting high wire act. He compellingly oscillated between callous brute, panic attack-prone psychiatrist patient, conflicted husband and father, and more. Complex vulnerability brewed beneath Tony's steely veneer. Gandolfini's acting choices granted the character a staggering 28 dimensions weekly.

He claimed three straight Emmy wins for Outstanding Lead Actor from 2000-2003, bookended by two other nominations in 1999 and 2007. Gandolfini also nabbed one SAG award for Outstanding Performance in 2000 alongside widespread nominations. And he had been awarded the coveted Television Critics Association honor twice by 2002.

While Chase earned worthy acclaim for his layered writing and filmic vision, he emphasized Gandolfini as the creative linchpin:

"Without James, this project never would have existed. The casting of that role was 90% of making the show."

Upon Gandolfini's sad demise in 2013, Chase expanded on sentiment:

"He was a genius. Anyone who saw him even in the smallest of his performances knows that. He is one of the greatest actors of this or any time."

The Sopranos revolutionized television. Chase relied on Gandolfini to manifest his vision for complexity previously unseen on the small screen. He consciously avoided storytelling formulas or simplification. Instead he channeled cinema giants like Coppola, Scorsese and Kazan exploring psychological depth. Gandolfini unlocked that, his skill overcoming any commercial reservations over an antihero carrying serialized content.

Chase repeatedly praised Gandolfini's daring creative contributions, collaborating over rewrites to harvest striking acting moments. Their symbiosis enabled transcendent viewing and mainstream acceptance of flawed lead characters. Tony Soprano battled psychiatry-treated panic attacks, brooding depression, hedonistic tendencies and homicidal ruthlessness all while the audience ROOTED for his survival. This represented Gandolfini's genius.

Traces of Tony's conflicted DNA now appear across modern antiheroes. Similar dynamics drive storylines for characters like Breaking Bad's Walter White, Mad Men's Don Draper, Boardwalk Empire's Nucky Thompson and Dexter Morgan of his eponymous series. Each descends morally ambiguous arcs while still earning viewer empathy. Gandolfini pioneered this through acting brilliance deserving recognition alongside Chase's writing and vision.

Select Gandolfini performances are in public memory for their authentic emotional resonance. After disagreements over Meadow's college choice, Tony tears up realizing he'll lose his daughter. When Uncle Junior's advancing dementia prevents him from remembering a shared childhood memory, Tony breaks down at his beloved elder's deteriorating state.

Upon discovering his best friend Big Pussy wears a wire for the FBI, Tony strangles him. The devastating betrayal etched across

Gandolfini's face telegraphs immense hurt. Later when Tony escapes assassination by the skin of his teeth, Gandolfini collapses against a wall, heaving frantic gulps of air as survival adrenaline courses through his body.

Tony's most explosive eruptions also hold unshakeable staying power thanks to Gandolfini's terrifying conviction. When restaurant hostess Meadow brings home an African-American boyfriend, Tony physically throws her across the room in revulsion. He also unleashes on his therapist Dr. Melfi, screaming she helped enable his crimes by failing to stop him. Both scenes viscerally resonate as Gandolfini occupies disturbing spaces rife with rage.

But Gandolfini's crowning scene happens when Tony enters a dream state after his friend is gunned down. He envisions an afterlife where entering a country inn symbolizes the point of no return. Tony searches for assurance he led a worthy life but only feels the weight of sin.

When Gandolfini pleads "I get it!" upon seeing vision after vision alluding to karmic judgment awaiting, his beautiful acting reflects true fear over the cost of choices.

Chapter 6: The Tragic End

On June 19, 2013, Gandolfini suffered a fatal heart attack while vacationing in Rome ahead of a nearby Sicilian film festival appearance. His 13-year old son Michael discovered him collapsed inside the extravagant Boscolo Exedra Roma bathroom after his father failed to join the family for a Tuscan countryside excursion.

Hotel staff and emergency responders rushed to try reviving the star to no avail. Gandolfini experienced cardiac arrest stemming from heart disease and died that evening at 51 despite medics' valiant attempts at resuscitation.

News swiftly shocked the entertainment world with glowing tributes pouring forth instantly. Broad sadness reigned that such a gifted actor perished so prematurely at the height of creative prowess. Unanswered questions lingered about projects left unfinished from an undeniable force still reaching full potential.

While Gandolfini's messy struggles and excesses no doubt contributed to his untimely demise, toxicology tests found no evidence of substances at the time of death. Hotel records instead indicated his final evening involved normal dining with Tom Richardson, his assistant and documentarian chosen to capture Gandolfini's Italy visit on film for potential future use.

Richardson provided initial public details about Gandolfini's haunting last breaths, having accompanied Michael after he discovered his father keeled over in the locked bathroom. The apparent documented initial revival efforts by on-site nurses until paramedics whisked Gandolfini to Policlinico Umberto I hospital where tireless doctors could not outrace the tragedy.

When media reached Richardson, he emphasized Gandolfini exhibited no prior signs of ill health that fatal evening, seen happily posing for fan photographs earlier at the hotel's bar. They enjoyed a fine relaxing dinner on the outdoor terrace under Roman moonlight recounting stories from set before Gandolfini retired around 10 p.m. with plans to rise early driving to Sicily. Tragically, he never saw sunrise.

Italian authorities conducted an extensive autopsy seeking clues behind the shocking loss of a beloved star while vacationing in their country. The results confirmed Gandolfini's cause of death as natural despite widespread early speculation regarding relapse or overdose.

The findings included severe coronary artery disease caused by years of unhealthy habits despite Gandolfini slimming down in recent seasons. Plaque discovered lining the actor's circulatory system triggered lethal arrhythmia and cardiac arrest once a significant blockage prevented sufficient oxygen-rich blood reaching his heart.

Gandolfini's years of heavy drinking and smoking no doubt accelerated the plaque accumulation, taxing the organ over time. Traces of prescription drugs were detected but at normal levels having been taken correctly for ongoing conditions. No illicit substances were present.

The medical examiner summarized Gandolfini simply as "a healthy man whose heart killed him." While loved ones including his second wife Deborah Lin and sister Leta felt devastated by his loss, toxicology findings eased initial distress over imagining a consciously self-destructive relapse ending Gandolfini's life.

Instead, the tragedy reflected long-term repercussions from prior coping habits. Gandolfini neither fatally overdosed intentionally nor harbored hidden addictions reignited despite 14 months of sobriety. Unaware of any lingering cardiovascular damage, his heart sadly gave out fully by chance rather than choice.

On June 27th 2013 at Manhattan's Cathedral Church of Saint John the Divine, 2,000 friends, family members, co-stars, Hollywood admirers and adoring fans gathered honoring James Gandolfini's incredible life and career during an elegant state funeral.

Heartfelt, humor-filled eulogies from Gandolfini's widow Lin, Sopranos creator David Chase and colleague Thomas Richardson painted a picture of a fiercely loyal friend who nurtured deep bonds. Yes, he engendered occasional frustration and chaos through turbulent battles with addiction. But those who truly knew Gandolfini referenced his earnest warmth, fierce insight into the human condition and relentless commitment toward his craft.

While many offered condolences, Gandolfini's loved ones expressed comfort in how he cherished the later years spending time with his children, finding stability with Lin and enjoying revived zeal producing historical documentaries and supporting veteran charities between acting roles. Private struggles never fully disappeared, but career purpose and deepening personal contentment endured near the end.

Chase affectionately emphasized how Gandolfini's profound talent changed television. Lin shared intimate moments conveying Gandolfini's intellect and passion for life at home. Richardson revealed behind-the-scenes devotion between the actor and Sopranos crew members who considered him extended family.

These meaningful perspectives reinforced Gandolfini's multilayered legacy. He revolutionized acting standards across an ascendant medium through tour de force execution. He enabled groundbreaking creative heights envisioning an antihero character embracing mental health struggles traditionally receiving only stigmatic portrayals.

Yes, Gandolfini fell victim to near mythic personal demons off-screen. However, his work ethic, philosophy and loyalty in stewarding

Sopranos' success while battling those demons still inspired universal praise.

Eulogizers conveyed Gandolfini wrestled daily against inner anguish to deliver excellence. They emphasized that rather than excuse such struggles, Gandolfini instead channeled emotional truth to inform captivating acting. This aligned with Chase's final assessment of his irreplaceable star's uncommon gift bridling turmoil into dramatic achievement:

"He had the deepest sensitivity to finding that truth, with no hijinks or shtick. In looking for truth, he examined every region of his life...The pathetic, the sad, the rage. And he used these feelings to inform his work. God gave Jimmy that gift."

Printed in Great Britain
by Amazon

37921700R00026